FOAL

JUNIOR
BIOGRAPHY
FROM
ANCIENT
CIVILIZATIONS

CONFUCIUS

RUSSELL ROBERTS

Mitchell Lane
PUBLISHERS

P.O. Box 196
Hockessin, Delaware 19707
Visit us on the web: www.mitchelllane.com
Comments? Email us: mitchelllane@mitchelllane.com

JUNIOR
BIOGRAPHY
FROM

ANCIENT CIVILIZATIONS

Alexander the Great • Archimedes
Augustus Caesar • Confucius • Genghis Khan
Homer • Leif Erikson • Marco Polo
Nero • Socrates

Copyright © 2014 by Mitchell Lane
Publishers

ABOUT THE AUTHOR: Russell Roberts has
written and published nearly 40 books
for adults and children, including *C.C.
Sabathia, Larry Fitzgerald, The Building of
the Panama Canal, The Cyclopes, The
Minotaur, Scott Joplin,* and *The Battle of
Waterloo.* He lives in Bordentown, New
Jersey, with his family and a fat, fuzzy, and
crafty calico cat named Rusti.

PUBLISHER'S NOTE: The facts on which
the story in this book is based have been
thoroughly researched. Documentation
of such research can be found on pages
44–45. While every possible effort has been
made to ensure accuracy, the publisher
will not assume liability for damages
caused by inaccuracies in the data, and
makes no warranty on the accuracy of the
information contained herein.

Printing 1   2   3   4   5   6   7   8   9

Library of Congress
Cataloging-in-Publication Data

Roberts, Russell, 1953–
 Confucius / by Russell Roberts.
    pages cm. — (Junior biography from
ancient civilizations)
 Includes bibliographical references and
index.
 ISBN 978-1-61228-436-1 (library bound)
1. Confucius—Juvenile literature. 2.
Philosophers—China—Biography—Juvenile
literature. I. Title.
 B128.C8R63 2013
 181'.112—dc23
 [B]
                                          2013012552

eBook ISBN: 9781612284989

                                          PLB

CONTENTS

Chapter One
The Party That Wasn't 5
Socrates 9

Chapter Two
The Young Master 11
China in the Time of Confucius 15

Chapter Three
An Intellectual Man 17
The Rooster and the Mustard 21

Chapter Four
In Public Service 23
The Changing Role of the Merchant......25

Chapter Five
Wandering......................................27
In the Words of Confucius....................37

Chronology 40

Timeline 42

Chapter Notes 43

Further Reading 44
    Works Consulted............................44
    On the Internet 45

Phonetic Pronunciations 46

Glossary...47

Index 48

Phonetic pronunciations of words in **bold**
can be found on page 46.

Like all pictures of Confucius, this one of him as Minister of Justice is just a guess, since no actual images of what he really looked like are known to exist.

CHAPTER 1
The Party That Wasn't

It was supposed to be a festive occasion . . . but it filled **Confucius*** with terror.

It was the spring of 500 BCE (Before the Common Era). Confucius was the Minister of Justice for his master, Duke Ting, who was head of the Chinese state of **Lu**. Confucius's advice to the Duke had been so good that Lu had prospered.

However, Lu's prosperity did not please everyone. Duke Ching, ruler of the neighboring state of **Ch'i**, was worried about Lu's continued good fortune. He had taken several fortresses and small territories on the border between the two states. He feared that Lu would want to retake them. So Duke Ching plotted against Lu.

Ting was not smart. He happily accepted an invitation from Ching to meet with him near the border and discuss state matters. Ting even considered going alone.

Confucius was suspicious. He told his master that if he wanted peace he should prepare for war—advice still followed by rulers of countries thousands of years later. Confucius convinced Duke Ting to take a royal procession with him to

*For pronunciations of words in **bold**, see page 46.

the meeting. The procession would include ministers (including Confucius), dignitaries, and guards. Ting agreed.

Upon arriving at the meeting place, Ting discovered that Ching was already there and had brought many of his own people. If Ting had come alone, he would have been outnumbered.

Confucius and Ting discovered that Ching had built a special structure. It had a platform on top, where the two rulers would sit and talk. Confucius suspected trouble.

The two rulers climbed the stairs to the platform and began their meeting as Confucius nervously watched. Then a Ch'i official went up the stairs and asked Ching to allow some music to be performed. Moments later, barbarians disguised as dancers in wild costumes with animal feathers and tails appeared. They began yelling and screaming, beating drums and waving sticks. As the dancers moved closer to the Lu officials, Confucius saw that they were carrying weapons such as spears and swords.

Everyone from Lu was in great danger!

Quickly Confucius scrambled up the steps. He told Duke Ching that barbarians had no business interrupting a meeting of noble Chinese princes. He asked that they be removed.

Ching, embarrassed that Confucius had uncovered his trick, immediately ordered the "dancers" to go away. But he wasn't finished. Soon the meeting ground was filled with circus performers. There were jugglers tossing clubs into the air, acrobats rolling and tumbling, and dancers leaping about. Confucius suspected another trick. Once again he hustled up the stairs to the two rulers. "When vile fellows disturb a conference of their lords, they deserve to be chastised [punished],"[1] he said.

By now Duke Ching was ready to die of embarrassment. Twice Confucius had foiled his plans. He stormed down the stairs to his officials and yelled at them for recommending that he bring dancers and circus performers.

Trickery and deceit were common among the leaders of the Chinese states. Even such an innocent-looking thing as dancing could turn deadly in a moment, which is why everyone had to be on their guard at all times.

To cover his shame, Duke Ching returned the border territories and fortresses back to Duke Ting. Confucius had won a great victory for Lu.

Unfortunately, Confucius couldn't enjoy his victory for very long. Soon he would be forced to leave Lu.

全国重点文物保护单位

曲阜鲁国故城

中华人民共和国国务院
一九六一年三月四日公布

Confucius was born in the Chinese state of Lu, at a time of warfare between the states. They often used walls to protect important places, such as this small section of wall from Lu's capital city.

Socrates

Like Confucius, the great Greek philosopher **Socrates** has influenced how people think and act.

Socrates is thought to have been born in 469 BCE in the city-state of Athens. His father was a sculptor named **Sophroniscus** and his mother was named **Phaenarete**. Socrates fought in several battles during the Peloponnesian War, a conflict among Greek city-states.

Little else is known of Socrates' personal life. He married a woman named **Xanthippe**, and they had three sons. Nevertheless, the two did not get along well. Socrates is supposed to have said that after learning to live with Xanthippe he could get along with anyone.

The most famous story about Socrates concerns his death in 399 BCE. He was tried and convicted of corrupting the youth of Athens and of not believing in the official gods. Asked what he thought his punishment should be, he sarcastically suggested free dinners and a government wage. He was instead ordered to commit suicide by drinking hemlock.

Even though he did not write down any of his teachings, others did. The most notable was his student Plato, who developed the Socratic Method. It is still used today. It basically means that to find answers, one must question everything.

The Death of Socrates, by Jacques-Louis David (1787)

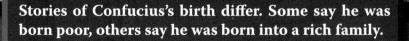

至聖孔子

兗州府曲阜縣人

名丘字仲尼山東

Stories of Confucius's birth differ. Some say he was born poor, others say he was born into a rich family.

CHAPTER 2
The Young Master

Some of what is known about Confucius's life comes from a book called *Records of the Grand Historian* by Sima Qian, who lived from 145 to 85 BCE. Another book that contains details about Confucius and his teachings is *The Analects*. However, both of these books were written many years after Confucius lived. So it is almost impossible to tell what is accurate and what is not about Confucius's life. In addition, there are elements of myth in accounts of Confucius's life.

He was born in late September, 551 BCE, in the town of **Tsou**, which was in the Chinese state of Lu. His father's name was **Shu-Liang Ho**. His mother's name is unknown. According to many stories, Shu-Liang Ho was around 70 years old when his son was born. He was a retired soldier.

Shu-Liang Ho had nine other children—all daughters—with his wife, and a clubfooted son by another woman. However, in Chinese society males were very important, and females were not. Sons performed the sacred rituals after their father's death, so his spirit would be content. Shu-Liang Ho's only male child was a cripple—an imperfect son. So he convinced a family named Yan to let him try to have a child with their teenage daughter.[1]

According to the legend, the couple made love in the fields, then went to a sacred mountain named **Ni** and prayed. Another story says that Confucius's mother, while pregnant, was walking in the woods one day when she met a unicorn. The animal gave her a piece of jade. An inscription on the jade revealed the great wisdom her still-unborn son would possess. She knew this was a good omen from the gods. She tied a white ribbon around one of its horns.

When he was born, Confucius was named **K'ung Chung-Ni**. As he got older he was known as Master K'ung, or **K'ung Fu-tze**. When Jesuit priests arrived in China many centuries after his death and first encountered this name, they pronounced and spelled it the way it sounded to them: Confucius.

Shu-Liang Ho died when Confucius was just three years old. His death took away any income that Confucius and his mother enjoyed, and the two of them had a hard time getting by. "I was of humble status,"[2] Confucius said of his childhood.

The mother of Confucius enlisted the aid of spiritual forces at a divine mountain to ensure that she would have a son, and was rewarded not just with a male, but one that a unicorn announced would be special.

According to some accounts, Confucius grew to be over six feet tall.[3] This would agree with a description of his father as a large man. Although not very much is known about Confucius's studies, he enjoyed the process of learning very much. He felt that people should never stop trying to learn because education was the key to success.

Confucius's humble origins gave him a connection with the common people that would never leave him. Many of the people in China of that time were peasants, and Confucius always remembered that he was one of them. However, this meant that it was going to be hard for Confucius to get a good job. These positions were mostly reserved for children of prominent families.

Confucius did not want a lowly job. However, since it was the only avenue available to him, Confucius decided to take some of these menial jobs and work his way up the ladder. He was ambitious, and knew this method was his best chance to achieve fame and fortune.

Lu was one of numerous states in China at this time. These states were constantly at war with each other. Because it was small and weak, Lu could have easily been swallowed up by one of the larger states. Yet Lu was also considered a place in which the ancient rites, culture, and ceremonies were being preserved, and this likely saved it. It would not have looked good for another state to destroy tradition-filled Lu. Nevertheless, Lu still suffered 21 invasions during the chaotic years of the Spring and Warring periods (722–481 BCE).[4]

Confucius thought that people needed rituals and ceremonies to help forge a strong society, and that rulers needed to follow rituals so that they could govern people kindly. He felt a return to the old ways would help end the violence of the current times.

The Chi family, one of the three powerful families in Lu, took notice of Confucius. They gave him work in the accounting office of one of their grain facilities. Next he oversaw the Chi family's animal flocks and grazing grounds.

Steppes
Yellow river
Yan
Ji (Beijing)
(Tianjin)
Bohai Sea
Korean Penisula
Qi
(Jinan)
Linzi
Jin
Yellow river
Wei
Yi Kaifeng Chiqiu
(Zhengzhou)
Qin
Yong
Wei river
Zhou
Lu
Qufu
Yellow Sea
(Xi'an)
Cao
Chengpu
Chengzhou
Zheng Shangqiu
Song
Chen
Shangcai
Cai
Huai river
Chu
Wu
East China Sea
Legend
(Nanjing) (Shanghai)
(Hefei) Gusu
Sichuan Basin
(Hangzou)
Ying (Wuhan)
Guiji
Yanzi river
Southern hills

Qin State
☆ Imperial capital
◎ State's capital
● Ancient or (modern) city
Physical item
Yellow
Rivers

Before it was one country, China was comprised of many different states, which often warred with each other. This was the situation Confucius was born into.

However, Confucius was far more suited for teaching and philosophy. All his life Confucius wanted to become famous and help the common people. The best way to do that was to have an important government job. There he could influence the way things were done and hopefully cause positive change.

Confucius spent much of his time reading and studying. Soon he was recognized by others as a wise man. He likely became a leader and teacher quite by accident. As Confucius biographer H.G. Creel writes, "Probably the first students were simply a group of friends. . . . This is borne out by the fact that some of the disciples were only a little younger than Confucius."[5]

Both his education and his intellect made Confucius a natural leader. He had taken his first steps toward his dream—fame.

China in the Time of Confucius

China was a very different place in Confucius's time than it is today.

First of all, it was not called "China." The name "China" came into being during the reign of the First Emperor, **Qin Shihangdi** (221–210 BCE), because he was from the state of Chin. Qin Shihangdi unified the various states of China into a single country and named it after his state.

At the time Confucius lived, the fabric of Chinese society was fraying, because of the constant wars. Formerly, political divisions had centered around prominent families. The peasants worked the land for their particular family and gave them much of the crops they grew. In exchange, the family protected the peasants from invaders.

Qin Shihangdi

When Confucius was young, this system still existed, and people felt safe and protected. During his lifetime, however, this system gradually disintegrated, the power of the families weakened, and war and conflict spread over the land.

The rules of etiquette and ritual were also falling apart during Confucius's time. These rules dictated the way people acted and interacted with each other. By the time Confucius was grown, they had largely been abandoned. Confucius tried to restore the role of ritual and tradition in Chinese life.

"Everything has its beauty, but not everyone sees it," Confucius said. He may have been referring to himself. By all reports, his physical appearance wasn't very attractive.

CHAPTER 3
An Intellectual Man

Confucius got married when he was 19 years old. The full name of his wife is not known, only that she was from a family with the name of Kien-kuan. A year later, his wife gave birth to a boy. To celebrate the event Duke Chao, the ruler of Lu, sent Confucius a carp (a type of fish) as a gift.[1] Confucius called the boy **Li**, meaning carp. At some point Confucius also became the father of a daughter. Unfortunately, Confucius did not stay married long, although it is not known why.

Confucius was not a handsome man. He had an indentation in the center of his head. As a result, the sides of his skull were slightly higher than the middle. He also had a large and unattractive nose with warts on it. His upper teeth were very prominent. His front teeth stuck out and hung over his bottom lip.

In 528 BCE Confucius's mother died. Confucius buried her in a temporary grave, then found the grave of his father and re-buried his mother next to him. As was the custom in China, he mourned her for three years. Then he opened a school. He taught music, poetry, history, and ritual. He was especially concerned that his students learned moral values.

As he entered his late 20s, Confucius's life was not going as he had hoped. One event in particular defined his position in Chinese society. The head of the powerful and influential Ki family gave a banquet and invited all men of importance. Without an invitation Confucius should have stayed away, but he went anyway and presented himself at the door. A man named Yang Hu answered the door and looked at Confucius. "The head of the Ki family is giving a banquet to men of rank," Yang Hu said. "He would not demean himself to give you a banquet."[2] Embarrassed, Confucius left.

When Confucius was 34, the Duke of Chao was the ruler of Lu. However, the real power in Lu was three rich families: Chi, Meng, and Shu. The Duke tried to overthrow one of the heads of these families, Baron P'ing. However, the other families sent troops to support Baron P'ing and the Duke was forced to flee to the neighboring state of Ch'i. One of Confucius's core beliefs was that the rightful central authority (the government or the leader of the government) must be obeyed no matter what happened. So Confucius went into exile in Ch'i as well.

The ruler of Ch'i, Duke Ching, decided Confucius was the perfect person to govern some of the land in his country. However, one of Duke Ching's advisers talked him out of the idea, and no job was offered to Confucius.

About 509 BCE Duke Chao died. His younger brother Ting was allowed to return to Lu as Duke. Confucius also returned.

A few years later, Yang Hu (the same man who had spoken so disrespectfully to Confucius years before) became head of Lu through trickery and violence. He asked Confucius to see him. Confucius considered Yang Hu nothing more than a crude bandit and refused the invitation. Yang Hu sent Confucius the gift of a fat pig, which meant that Confucius had to pay him a visit and thank him. Confucius

Confucius enjoyed music, both listening to it and playing it. "Music produces a kind of pleasure which human nature cannot do without," he said.

When Confucius was middle-aged, his sense of duty and honor caused him to travel throughout China.

did indeed visit Yang Hu—but went at a time when he knew Yang Hu was not home.

Then Yang Hu let it be known that he intended to offer Confucius a public service position. It was what Confucius had always wanted. Yet his loyalties were to Duke Ting, who by ritual and tradition was the rightful leader of Lu. So Confucius kept putting off accepting the offer.

Finally, one day Yang Hu said to him, "Does he who takes an interest in public affairs and lets opportunities to guide them pass by deserve to be called prudent? The days and the months go by, the years do not wait for us."[3]

Confucius answered, "Very well. I will accept a post."[4] However, before he could actually take the job, Yang Hu's government was overthrown in 502 BCE and the leader fled.

It was now that Fortune was finally ready to smile on Confucius.

The Rooster and the Mustard

During this time, one of the sports enjoyed in China was cockfighting—two roosters fighting to the death. The Duke of Chao and Baron P'ing, who was head of one of Lu's powerful families and whose support helped keep Chao in power, decided to have a cockfight with two of their roosters. During the contest, an argument erupted between the two men. It seems that P'ing had put mustard on his rooster's wings so it might get it in the other rooster's eyes and blind him. However, Chao had also cheated, putting metal on his rooster's toes so the bird could better slash his opponent.

The Duke of Chao gathered an army with the help of some of Lu's other families. He launched a surprise attack on the fortress of Baron P'ing.

At first the Duke's soldiers forced Baron P'ing to retreat into a tower of his fortress. From here he tried to negotiate with the Duke of Chao. The Duke, however, did not listen. When Baron P'ing saw this, he turned to some of the other families who were helping Chao against him. If I am defeated, P'ing said to them, how long do you think it will be until Chao attacks you as well?

The other families turned their armies against Chao. He fled Lu one step ahead of the armies, proving that, despite the old saying, birds of a feather don't necessarily always flock together.

Three great philosophers, leaders and teachers: Laozi (the founder of Taoism) is on the left. Confucius (right) holds Gautama Buddha, the founder of Buddhism.

CHAPTER 4
In Public Service

After Yang Hu's forced departure, Lu was in chaos. Eventually all of the rich families backed one person as leader: Duke Ting. However, Ting desperately needed someone he could rely on for advice and help. That person was Confucius.

So, in 501 BCE, at the age of 50, Confucius finally received the government post he had long sought. He was appointed governor of **Chong-tu**, an area in the middle of Lu. Confucius made sure that everyone had enough food, levied taxes fairly, and established a system of measurements.

Confucius did such a good job as governor that Duke Ting asked if the rest of Lu could be governed like that. When Confucius replied "yes," Ting promoted him first to Minister of Public Works and then to Minister of Justice, where he saved Ting during the meeting with Duke Ching.

One of Confucius's great accomplishments was lessening the power of the ruling families by persuading them to demolish their fortresses. That way their troops could not be used in a rebellion against Duke Ting.

Confucius was friendly and straightforward, yet somewhat shy. When he spoke he bent forward slightly. He had a broad face with a wide mouth, and a thick, full beard. His complexion was dark. He did not like to dress in colorful clothing, so he almost always wore black. He loved music and was frightened of thunder.

Before Confucius would eat rice, it had to be very well cleaned. His meat was always cut into very small pieces. In fact, he liked everything cut into pieces of the same size. He always made sure to eat vegetables with his meat. Before he ate, he first offered a small sacrifice to his ancestors.

Lu was prospering with Confucius. However, the neighboring district of **Ts'i** (also written as **Qi**) watched Lu with growing alarm. They did not want Lu to get too strong. They decided to anger Confucius so much that he would leave Lu.

The rulers of Ts'i trained 80 pretty girls as dancers and dressed them in beautiful clothes. They sent the women and 60 pairs of prize horses to Duke Ting as a gift.[1] Ting spent the whole day with the girls, neglecting all official business. According to some sources, Ting lingered for three days with the girls.[2]

One of Confucius's disciples urged his master to leave Duke Ting and go find someone else who was more serious about his official state duties. Although Confucius was deeply committed to the importance of performing state duties and ancient rituals when and as they should be done, he decided to give his ruler one more chance. There was an important sacrifice coming up. "If our ruler shares portions of the sacrificial meat with the court officers [as should have been done], then I will stay,"[3] Confucius said.

Unfortunately Duke Ting did not share portions of the sacrificial meat. Confucius resigned his official post and left Lu in 497 BCE. Many of his followers went with him. The years of wandering had begun.

The Changing Role of the Merchant

During the time of Confucius, the role of the Chinese merchant was changing.

Confucius had a disciple named **Zigong**, who desired a career in politics. One hundred years before it would not have been possible. Then, a merchant found goods that could not be found locally, and the rich families bought them and thus supported the merchants.

However, when the power of the wealthy families broke down, they could no longer support the merchants. So the merchants began hauling their goods along China's extensive road system and selling them to the people they met. As the merchants traveled they saw things that not many other people saw. Thus they became spies and informants who possessed valuable information. As they became more important citizens in Chinese society, some merchants began to be available as candidates for high political office. Some men of high political office even resigned their office and became merchants themselves.

Painting of a merchant selling medicinal remedies such as bones, plants, and powders

The three great philosophers—Confucius (left), Laozi (center), and Buddha—never actually met, but their teachings and wisdom have influenced millions of people from all over the world.

CHAPTER 5
Wandering

When Confucius and his disciples first left Lu, they went northwest, toward the neighboring state of **Wei**. That night, at a city on the border between the two states, Confucius and his party had a visitor. After talking to Confucius, the visitor was leaving when he noticed how sad and depressed all of the disciples were.

"Why do you grieve at your master's loss of his post?" he said to them. "The world has long since lost its way. Heaven is using your master as a bell with a wooden clapper to warn the people."[1]

The next day Confucius entered Wei. With him were some of his favorite disciples, including his best friend **Tze** Lu, Tze Kung, and **Yen Hui**. Duke Ling, ruler of Wei, asked Confucius how much he had been paid in Lu, and Confucius replied that he had received 60,000 bushels of grain. The duke said that he would give him the same amount. Confucius believed he was in line for a government job.

At the court of Duke Ling was a notorious woman named **Nan Tze**, who had a bad reputation. She summoned Confucius to see her. Although

Confucius always felt that he would make more of an impact performing a government job, but it was in his teachings to his disciples that he and his wisdom have lived on.

he did not want to go, Confucius knew that he could not refuse because the duke liked her. He did not tell any of his disciples where he was going.

When Confucius arrived, Nan Tze was sitting behind a curtain. Confucius bowed, then stood in front of the curtain as she examined him through a hole in it. Eventually Confucius bowed again and left. However, when he returned to his lodgings Confucius found that his disciples were very upset over his visit. What would people say?

"I did not want to see her, but . . . had to pay her a visit," Confucius said. "If I have done anything wrong, may Heaven forsake me, may Heaven forsake me!"[2]

Soon after his visit to Nan Tze, word spread that Confucius was not to be trusted. One day Duke Ling asked Confucius to go riding. However, when Confucius showed up there were two carriages. The

Court visits could be very elaborate affairs, as both the guest and the host tried to impress each other. However, being a simple man, Confucius usually just visited all by himself.

During his years of wandering, Confucius went all over China, using whatever form of transportation he could find—ox cart, chariot, and walking when all else failed.

Duke and Nan Tze were in the first carriage, while Confucius was forced to follow in the second. Now Confucius knew that Duke Ling did not trust him, and would never give him a public service job.

"I have yet to meet a man who loved virtue as much as outer splendor,"[3] Confucius said sadly. He and his followers left Wei.

Confucius spent the rest of the time that he was wandering about China in search of a prince or royal family who would employ him in government. However, even though many princes and important people asked him questions about government, no one offered him a job.

It was not hard to see why. Wars and violence were commonplace in China. Constant wars enabled the princes to gain more territory. Why would anyone want to employ Confucius, who hated war and told everyone how it made the common people suffer.

China was a dangerous country to travel around in. At one point Confucius was confused with a bandit. He and most of his followers were thrown into prison. Yen Hui, however, was not among them. Finally, after five days Yen Hui arrived to get Confucius out of prison.

"I thought you were dead!"[4] Confucius said in relief.

"O Master, as long as you are alive, how can I dare to die?"[5] answered Yen Hui.

Eventually Confucius returned to Wei. He was in his mid-sixties, and he felt very much a failure. Except for a brief time, he had not used his talents for public service. People had imprisoned him and shown him dishonor.

Wei was now run by Duke Cho. However, even though Duke Cho wanted Confucius to be his advisor, Confucius refused to have anything do with him because he thought he was a dishonorable man.

Finally, Confucius returned to his beloved state of Lu, probably about 484 BCE. He was in his late 60s, and had been wandering for 14 years. Two of the most powerful men in Lu were Duke **Ngai** and **Ki Kang**. Although they talked with Confucius, they did not offer

"Old age, believe me, is a good and pleasant thing," said Confucius, and he remained a teacher and philosopher as he grew older.

him a job. They were interested in power and money, and did not want to hear somebody tell them how to act with advice like "The virtue of the prince is that of the wind; the virtue of the people is that of the grass. The grass bends in the direction of the wind."[6]

In the spring of 480 BCE a member of Duke Ngai's hunting party captured a mysterious animal. Confucius was asked to identify it. He knew immediately that it was the unicorn that had appeared to his mother before his birth. It still had the ribbon around one of its horns that his mother had tied there.

Long ago the unicorn had announced Confucius's birth. Now it had returned to announce his death. Confucius covered his face and cried.

However, Confucius did not die just then. He lived for another year. One day in 479 BCE, he awoke early and told one of his followers that he had just had a dream in which he was sitting between two pillars used in a ceremony that gave sacrifices to the dead. Then Confucius lay back down, and never got up again. Seven days later he died. He was 72 years old.

Confucius was buried near the **Sishui** River. A temple was built at the site. Many of his belongings, such as his chariot, his hat, and his lute—his favorite musical instrument—were placed inside. His disciples mourned his death for three years.

In time the words of Confucius would become a beacon by which people would try to live their lives. The man who had sometimes felt that his life had been a failure had achieved everlasting fame.

The entrance way to the tomb of Confucius is flanked by stone statues.

大成至聖文宣王

Supposedly the disciples of Confucius planted trees from their hometowns in the forest surrounding Confucius's tomb.

"Consideration of others is the basis of a good life, a good society."
—Confucius

In the Words of Confucius

Below are just a few of the best-known quotes from Confucius. There are many more.

1. Our greatest glory is not in never falling but in rising every time we fall.
2. Have no friends not equal to yourself.
3. Worry not that no one knows of you; seek to be worth knowing.
4. A man who has committed a mistake and doesn't correct it, is committing another mistake.
5. Before you embark on a journey of revenge, dig two graves.
6. Consideration for others is the basis of a good life, a good society.
7. Study the past if you would divine the future.
8. No matter where you go—there you are.
9. Life is really simple, but we insist on making it complicated.
10. Words are the voice of the heart.

During China's Song Dynasty (960–1279 A.D.), Confucius's philosophy became mixed with parts of Taoism and Buddhism and this combined philosophy was then used as the basis of student exams.

All Dates BCE

551	Confucius is born.
548	Confucius's father dies.
532	Confucius marries.
528	Confucius's mother dies.
517	Confucius goes into exile in the state of Ch'i out of a sense of duty.
509	Confucius returns to Lu.
501	Confucius becomes governor of Chung-tu.
500	Confucius foils the plot of Duke Ching.
497	Confucius leaves Lu, begins years of wandering.
484	Confucius returns to Lu.
479	Confucius dies.

Bronze statue of Confucius in Shiyang Town of Yunnan, China

大成殿

萬世師表

**Confucius Temple
in Shanghai, China**

All dates BCE

ca. 600	Chinese cultivate crops in rows, a technique not used in Europe until the 18th century A.D.
587	Nebuchadnezzar II destroys Jerusalem.
ca. 563	Buddha is born.
550	The rise of drama in Greece begins.
509	Rome turns out its last king and becomes a republic.
507	Athens (Greece) becomes a democracy.
499	War erupts between Persian Empire and Greece.
ca. 483	Buddha dies.
490	Athenians defeat Persian invaders at the Battle of Marathon.
469	Greek philosopher Socrates is born.
460	Birth of Hippocrates, "the Father of Medicine."
447	Athenians begin building the Parthenon; it is completed in 432.
ca. 400	Greek philosopher Democritus suggests that tiny particles called "atoms" make up the world.
399	Socrates dies after being forced to drink hemlock.
370	Hippocrates dies.

Chapter 1—The Party That Wasn't
1. Pierre Do-Dinh, *Confucius and Chinese Humanism* (New York: Funk & Wagnalls, 1969), p. 63.

Chapter 2—The Young Master
1. Annping Chin, *The Authentic Confucius* (New York: Scribner, 2007), p. 24.
2. H.G. Creel, *Confucius: The Man and the Myth* (New York: The John Day Company, 1949), p. 25.
3. Chin, *The Authentic Confucius*, p. 25.
4. Creel, *Confucius: The Man and the Myth*, p. 18.
5. Ibid, p. 29.

Chapter 3—An Intellectual Man
1. Pierre Do-Dinh, *Confucius and Chinese Humanism* (New York: Funk & Wagnalls, 1969), p. 29.
2. Ibid, p. 34.
3. Ibid, p. 58.
4. Ibid, p. 58.

Chapter 4—In Public Service
1. Annping Chin, *The Authentic Confucius* (New York: Scribner, 2007), p. 27.
2. Pierre Do-Dinh, *Confucius and Chinese Humanism* (New York: Funk & Wagnalls, 1969), p. 67.
3. Chin, *The Authentic Confucius*, p. 28.

Chapter 5—Wandering
1. Pierre Do-Dinh, *Confucius and Chinese Humanism* (New York: Funk & Wagnalls, 1969), p. 69.
2. Annping Chin, *The Authentic Confucius* (New York: Scribner, 2007), p. 90.
3. Do-Dinh, *Confucius and Chinese Humanism*, p. 72.
4. Ibid, p. 70.
5. Ibid, p. 70.
6. Ibid, p. 84.

Books

Burgan, Michael. *Confucius: Chinese Philosopher and Teacher*. Minneapolis, Minnesota: Compass Point Books, 2009.

Friedman, Mel. *Ancient China*. New York: Children's Press, 2010.

Johnson, Spencer. *A Value Tales Treasury: Stories for Growing Good People*. New York: Simon & Schuster, 2010.

Wang, Qicheng. *The Big Book of China: A Guided Tour Through 5,000 Years of History and Culture*. San Francisco, California: Long River Press, 2010.

Yen Mah, Adeline. *China: Land of Dragons and Emperors*. New York: Delacorte Books for Young Readers, 2009.

Works Consulted

Charles Moore, editor. *The Chinese Mind*. Honolulu, Hawaii: University of Hawaii Press, 1967.

Chin, Annping. *The Authentic Confucius*. New York: Scribner, 2007.

Confucius. *Confucius Analects*. Indianapolis, Indiana: Hackett Publishing Company, 2003.

Creel, H.G. *Confucius: The Man and the Myth*. New York: The John Day Company, 1949.

Dawson, Raymond. *Confucius*. New York: Hill and Wang, 1981.

Do-Dinh, Pierre. Confucius and Chinese Humanism. New York: Funk & Wagnalls, 1969.

Kaizuka, Shigeki. *Confucius*. New York: Macmillan, 1956.

On the Internet

New World Encyclopedia—"Socrates"

http://www.newworldencyclopedia.org/entry/Socrates

Tadlock, Catarina. "The Unicorn." The Ultimate Horse Site

http://www.ultimatehorsesite.com/info/horsemyths/
theunicorn.html

"Confucius Quotes." Great-Quotes.com

http://www.great-quotes.com/quotes/author//Confucius/pg/8

"Confucius." Chinese Philosophy for Kids.

http://www.historyforkids.org/learn/china/philosophy/
confucius.htm

Riegel, Jeffrey. "Confucius." Stanford Encyclopedia of
Philosophy.

http://plato.stanford.edu/entries/confucius/

"Confucius." Chinese Travel Guide.

http://www.travelchinaguide.com/intro/history/zhou/eastern/
confucius.htm

"Confucius." Encyclopedia Britannica.

http://www.britannica.com/EBchecked/topic/132184/
Confucius

"Who Was Confucius?" A China Family Adventure.

http://www.china-family-adventure.com/
who-was-confucius.html

PHONETIC PRONUNCIATIONS

Confucius (kuhn-FYOO-shus)
Chao (CHOW)
Ch'I (CHEE)
Ki (KEE)
Kien-kuan (kee-EHN koo-AWN)
Ki kang (kee KAANG)
K'ung Chung-Ni (koong choong NE)
K'ung Fu-tze (koong FOO-dzu)
Li (LEE)
Lu (LOO)
Nan Tze (NAAN ZEE)
Ngai (NYE)
Ni (NEE)
Phaenarete (feh-nuh-REE-tee)

P'ing (PING)
Qi (CHEE)
Qin Shihangdi (CHEEN shee-hang-DEE)
Shu-Liang Ho (shoo- HOE)
Sishui (see-SHWEE)
Socrates (SAWK-ruh-teez)
Sophroniscus (sawf-roe-NISS-kuss)
T'si (TSEE)
Tsou (zee-OH)
Tze (ZEE)
Xantippe (zan-THIH-pee)
Wei (WAY)
Yang Hu (YAHNG HOO)
Yen Hui (YEN WHAY)
Zigong (zuh-GAHNG)

Statue of Confucius in Yueyang, China, on the shore of Dongting Lake

adultery (uh-DULL-tuh-ree)—Sexual intercourse by one married person with someone other than his or her legal spouse.

arouse (uh-ROUZ)—To stir to action.

barbarian (bar-BARE-ee-uhn)—A person in a savage, primitive state.

borne (BORN)—To remain firm under a load.

clubfooted (CLUB-fuh-tuhd)—Deformity in which foot is twisted into an awkward position.

demean (dee-MEEN)—To lower in dignity.

etiquette (EH-tuh-kuht)—An accepted code of social behavior.

festive (FESS-tive)—Suitable for a happy occasion.

forsake (fohr-SAKE)—To abandon or quit.

hemlock (HEM-lock)—A poisonous herb.

notorious (no-TORE-ee-us)—Widely but unfavorably known.

prominent (PRAW-muh-nent)—Standing out, distinctive.

ritual (RICH-oo-uhl)—An established procedure for a ceremony.

splendor (SPLEN-dohr)—Magnificence.

vile (VIUL)—Very bad.

virtue (VUHR-choo)—Goodness.

Athens 9

Buddha 22, 26

Chao, Duke 17, 18, 21

Ch'i 5, 6, 18

Chi Family 13, 18

Ching, Duke 5–7, 18, 23

Cho, Duke 31

Confucius

    appearance 17, 24

    as Minister of Justice 4, 5, 23

    as teacher 14, 28, 32

    birth 11, 12

    death 33

    marriage 17

Ho, Shu-Liang 11–12

Hu, Yang 18, 20, 23

Hui, Yen 27, 31

Kang, Ki 31

Kien-kuan family 17

Ki Family 18

Kung, Tze 27

Laozi 22, 26

Li 17

Ling, Duke 27, 29, 31

Lu (state) 5, 6, 7, 11, 13, 17, 18, 20, 21, 23, 24, 27, 31

Lu, Tze 27

Ngai, Duke 31, 33

Ni 12

Phaenarete 9

P'ing, Baron 18, 21

Plato 9

Qian, Sima 11

Shihangdi, Qin 15

Sishui River 33

Socrates 9

Sophroniscus 9

Ting, Duke 5–7, 18, 20, 23–24

Ts'i 24

Tze, Nan 27, 28, 29, 31

unicorn 12, 33

Wei 27, 31

Xanthippe 9

Zigong 25